THE PRINCIPLES OF ANARCHISM

AND OTHER WRITINGS

LUCY PARSONS

CONTENTS

1

THE PRINCIPLES OF ANARCHISM

A LECTURE

1890

Comrades and Friends: I think I cannot open my address more appropriately than by stating my experience in my long connection with the reform movement.

It was during the great railroad strike of 1877 that I first became interested in what is known as the "Labor Question." I then thought as many thousands of earnest, sincere people think, that the aggregate power operating in human society, known as government, could be made an instrument in the hands of the oppressed to alleviate their sufferings. But a closer study of the origin, history and tendency of governments convinced me that this was a mistake.

I came to understand how organized governments used their concentrated power to retard progress by their ever-ready means of silencing the voice of discontent if raised in vigorous protest against the machinations of the scheming few, who always did, always will and always must rule in the councils of nations where majority rule is recognized as the only means of adjusting the affairs of the people.

I came to understand that such concentrated power can be always wielded in the interest of the few and at the expense of the many. Government in its last analysis is this power reduced to a science. Governments never lead; they follow progress. When the prison, stake or scaffold can no longer silence the voice of the protesting minority, progress moves on a step, but not until then.

I will state this contention in another way: I learned by close study that it made no difference what fair promises a political party, out of power, might make to the people in order to secure their confidence, when once securely established in control of the affairs of society that they were after all but human with all the human attributes of the politician. Among these are: First, to remain in power at all hazards; if not individually, then those holding essentially the same views as the administration must be kept in control. Second, in order to keep in power, it is necessary to build up a powerful machine; one strong enough to crush all opposition and silence all vigorous murmurs of discontent, or the party machine might be smashed and the party thereby lose control.

When I came to realize the faults, failings, shortcomings, aspirations and ambitions of fallible man, I concluded that it would not be the safest nor best policy for society, as a whole, to entrust the management of all its affairs, with all their manifold deviations and ramifications in the hands of finite man, to be managed by the party which happened to come into power, and therefore was the majority party, nor did it then, nor does it now make one particle of difference to me what a party, out of power may promise; it does not tend to allay my fears of a party, when entrenched and securely seated in power might do to crush opposition, and silence the voice of the minority, and thus retard the onward step of progress.

My mind is appalled at the thought of a political party having control of all the details that go to make up the sum total of our lives. Think of it for an instant, that the party in power shall have all authority to dictate the kind of books that shall be used in our schools and universities, government officials editing, printing, and circulating our literature, histories, magazines and press, to say nothing of the thousand and one activities of life that a people engage in, in a civilized society.

To my mind, the struggle for liberty is too

great and the few steps we have gained have been won at too great a sacrifice, for the great mass of the people of this 20th century to consent to turn over to any political party the management of our social and industrial affairs. For all who are at all familiar with history know that men will abuse power when they possess it. For these and other reasons, I, after careful study, and not through sentiment, turned from a sincere, earnest, political Socialist to the non-political phase of Socialism— Anarchism—because in its philosophy I believe I can find the proper conditions for the fullest development of the individual units in society, which can never be the case under government restrictions.

The philosophy of anarchism is included in the word "Liberty," yet it is comprehensive enough to include all things else that are conducive to progress. No barriers whatever to human progression, to thought, or investigation are placed by anarchism; nothing is considered so true or so certain, that future discoveries may not prove it false; therefore, it has but one infallible, unchangeable motto, "Freedom": Freedom to discover any truth, freedom to develop, to live naturally and fully. Other schools of thought are composed of crystallized ideas—principles that are caught and impaled between the planks of long platforms, and considered too sacred to be disturbed by a close investigation. In all other "issues" there is always a limit; some imaginary boundary line beyond which the searching mind dare not penetrate, lest some pet idea melt into a myth. But anarchism is the usher of science—the master of ceremonies to all forms of truth. It would remove all barriers between the human being and natural development. From the natural resources of the Earth, all artificial restrictions, that the body might be nurtured, and from universal truth, all bars of prejudice and superstition, that the mind may develop symmetrically.

Anarchists know that a long period of education must precede any great fundamental change in society, hence they do not believe in vote-begging, nor political campaigns, but rather in the development of self-thinking individuals.

We look away from government for relief, because we know that force (legalized) invades the personal liberty of man, seizes upon the natural elements and intervenes between man and natural laws; from this exercise of force through governments flows nearly all the misery, poverty, crime and confusion existing in society.

So, we perceive, there are actual, material barriers blockading the way. These must be removed. If we could hope they would melt away, or be voted or prayed into nothingness, we would be content to wait and vote and pray. But they are like great frowning rocks towering between us and a land of freedom, while the dark chasms of a hard-fought past yawn behind us. Crumbling they may be with their own weight and the decay of time, but to quietly stand under until they fall is to be buried in the crash. There is something to be done in a case like this—the rocks must be removed. Passivity while slavery is stealing over us is a crime. For the moment we must forget that we are anarchists—when the work is accomplished we may forget that we were revolutionists—hence most anarchists believe the coming change can only come through a revolution, because the possessing class will not allow a peaceful change to take place; still we are willing to work for peace at any price, except at the price of liberty.

And what of the glowing beyond that is so bright that those who grind the faces of the poor say it is a dream? It is no dream, it is the real, stripped of brain-distortions materialized into thrones and scaffolds, miters and guns. It is nature acting on her own interior laws as in all her other associations. It is a return to first principles; for were not the land, the water, the light, all free before governments took shape and form? In this free state we will again forget to think of these things as "property." It is real, for we, as a race, are growing up to it. The idea of less restriction and more liberty, and a confiding trust that nature is equal to her work, is permeating all modern thought.

From the dark years—not so long gone by—when it was generally believed that man's soul was totally depraved and every human impulse bad; when every action, every thought and every emotion was controlled and restricted; when the human frame, diseased, was bled, dosed, suffocated and kept as far from nature's remedies as possible; when the mind was seized upon and distorted before it had time to evolve a natural thought—from those days to these years the progress of this idea has been swift and steady. It is becoming more and more apparent that in every way we are "governed best where we are governed least."

Still unsatisfied perhaps, the inquirer seeks for details, for ways and means, and whys and wherefores. How will we go on like human beings—eating and sleeping, working and loving, exchanging and dealing—without government? So used have we become to "organized authority" in every department of life that ordinarily we cannot conceive of the most common-place avocations being carried on without their interference and "protection." But anarchism is not compelled to outline a complete organization of a free society. To do so with any assumption of authority would be to place another barrier in the way of coming generations. The best thought of today may become the useless vagary of tomorrow, and to crystallize it into a creed is to make it unwieldy.

We judge from experience that man is a gregarious animal, and instinctively affiliates with his kind—co-operates, unites in groups, works to better advantage combined with his fellow men than when alone. This would point to the formation of co-operative communities, of which our present trades-unions are embryonic patterns. Each branch of industry will no doubt have its own organization, regulations, leaders, etc.; it will institute methods of direct communication with every member of that industrial branch in the world, and establish equitable relations with all other branches. There would probably be conventions of industry which delegates would attend, and where they would transact such business as was necessary, adjourn and from that moment be delegates no longer, but simply members of a group. To remain permanent members of a continuous congress would be to establish a power that is certain sooner or later to be abused.

No great, central power, like a congress consisting of men who know nothing of their constituents' trades, interests, rights or duties, would be over the various organizations or groups; nor would they employ sheriffs, policemen, courts or jailers to enforce the conclusions arrived at while in session. The members of groups might profit by the knowledge gained through mutual interchange of thought afforded by conventions if they choose, but they will not be compelled to do so by any outside force.

Vested rights, privileges, charters, title deeds, upheld by all the paraphernalia of government—the visible symbol of power—such as prison, scaffold and armies, will have no existence. There can be no privileges bought or sold, and the transaction kept sacred at the point of the bayonet. Every man will stand on an equal footing with his brother in the race of life, and neither chains of economic thralldom nor menial drags of superstition shall handicap the one to the advantage of the other.

Property will lose a certain attribute which sanctifies it now. The absolute ownership of it—"the right to use or abuse"—will be abolished, and possession, use, will be the only title. It will be seen how impossible it would be for one person to "own" a million acres of land, without a title deed, backed by a government ready to protect the title at all hazards, even to the loss of thousands of lives. He could not use the million acres himself, nor could he wrest from its depths the possible resources it contains.

People have become so used to seeing the evidences of authority on every hand that most of them honestly believe that they would go utterly to the bad if it were not for the policeman's club or the soldier's bayonet. But the anarchist says, "Remove these evidences of brute force, and let man feel the revivifying influences of self-responsibility and self-control, and see how we will respond to these better influences."

The belief in a literal place of torment has nearly melted away; and instead of the direful results predicted, we have a higher and truer standard of manhood and womanhood. People do not care to go to the bad when they find they can as well as not. Individuals are unconscious of their own motives in doing good. While acting out their natures according to their surroundings and conditions, they still believe they are being kept in the right path by some outside power, some restraint thrown around them by church or state. So the objector believes that with the right to rebel and secede, sacred to him, he would forever be rebelling and seceding, thereby creating constant confusion and turmoil.

Is it probable that he *would*, merely for the reason that he *could* do so? Men are to a great extent creatures of habit, and grow to love associations; under reasonably good conditions, he would remain where he commences, if he wished to, and, if he did not, who has any natural right to force him into relations distasteful to him? Under the present order of affairs, persons do unite with societies and remain good, disinterested members for life, where the right to retire is always conceded.

What we anarchists contend for is a larger opportunity to develop the units in society, that mankind may possess the right as a sound being to develop that which is broadest, noblest, highest and best, unhandicapped by any centralized authority, where he shall have to wait for his permits to be signed, sealed, approved and handed down to him before he can engage in the active pursuits of life with his fellow being. We know that after all, as we grow more enlightened under this larger liberty, we will grow to care less and less for that exact distribution of material wealth, which, in our greed-nurtured senses, seems now so impossible to think upon carelessly. The man and woman of loftier intellects, in the present, think not so much of the riches to be gained by their efforts as of the good they can do for their fellow creatures.

There is an innate spring of healthy action in every human being who has not been crushed and pinched by poverty and drudgery from before his birth, that impels him onward and upward. He cannot be idle, if he would; it is as natural for him to develop, expand, and use the powers within him when not repressed, as it is for the rose to bloom in the sunlight and fling its fragrance on the passing breeze.

The grandest works of the past were never

performed for the sake of money. Who can measure the worth of a Shakespeare, an Angelo or Beethoven in dollars and cents? Agassiz said, "he had no time to make money," there were higher and better objects in life than that. And so will it be when humanity is once relieved from the pressing fear of starvation, want, and slavery, it will be concerned, less and less, about the ownership of vast accumulations of wealth. Such possessions would be but an annoyance and trouble. When two or three or four hours a day of easy, of healthful labor will produce all the comforts and luxuries one can use, and the opportunity to labor is never denied, people will become indifferent as to who owns the wealth they do not need.

Wealth will be below par, and it will be found that men and women will not accept it for pay, or be bribed by it to do what they would not willingly and naturally do without it. Some higher incentive must, and will, supersede the greed for gold. The involuntary aspiration born in man to make the most of one's self, to be loved and appreciated by one's fellow-beings, to "make the world better for having lived in it," will urge him on to nobler deeds than ever the sordid and selfish incentive of material gain has done.

If, in the present chaotic and shameful struggle for existence, when organized society offers a premium on greed, cruelty, and deceit, men can be found who stand aloof and almost alone in their determination to work for good rather than gold, who suffer want and persecution rather than desert principle, who can bravely walk to the scaffold for the good they can do humanity, what may we expect from men when freed from the grinding necessity of selling the better part of themselves for bread? The terrible conditions under which labor is performed, the awful alternative if one does not prostitute talent and morals in the service of mammon; and the power acquired with the wealth obtained by ever-so-unjust means, combine to make the conception of free and voluntary labor almost an impossible one.

And yet, there are examples of this principle even now. In a well-bred family each person has certain duties, which are performed cheerfully, and are not measured out and paid for according to some pre-determined standard; when the united members sit down to the well-filled table, the stronger do not scramble to get the most, while the weakest do without, or gather greedily around them more food than they can possibly consume. Each patiently and politely awaits his turn to be served, and leaves what he does not want; he is certain that when again hungry plenty of good food will be provided. This principle can be extended to include all society, when people are civilized enough to wish it.

Again, the utter impossibility of awarding to each an exact return for the amount of labor performed will render absolute communism a necessity sooner or later. The land and all it contains, without which labor cannot be exerted, belong to no one man, but to all alike. The inventions and discoveries of the past are the common inheritance of the coming generations; and when a man takes the tree that nature furnished free, and fashions it into a useful article, or a machine perfected and bequeathed to him by many past generations, who is to determine what proportion is his and his alone? Primitive man would have been a week fashioning a rude resemblance to the article with his clumsy tools, where the modern worker has occupied an hour. The finished article is of far more real value than the rude one made long ago, and yet the primitive man toiled the longest and hardest.

Who can determine with exact justice what is each one's due? There must come a time when we will cease trying. The Earth is so bountiful, so generous; man's brain is so active, his hands so restless, that wealth will spring like magic, ready for the use of the world's inhabitants. We will become as much ashamed to quarrel over its possession as we are now to squabble over the food spread before us on a loaded table.

"But all this," the objector urges, "is very beautiful in the far off future, when we become angels. It would not do now to abolish govern-

ments and legal restraints; people are not pre-
pared for it."

This is a question. We have seen, in reading
history, that wherever an old-time restriction has
been removed the people have not abused their
newer liberty. Once it was considered necessary to
compel men to save their souls, with the aid of
governmental scaffolds, church racks and stakes.
Until the foundation of the American republic it
was considered absolutely essential that governments should second the efforts of the church in
forcing people to attend the means of grace; and
yet it is found that the standard of morals among
the masses is raised since they are left free to pray
as they see fit, or not at all, if they prefer it. It was
believed the chattel slaves would not work if the
overseer and whip were removed; they are so much
more a source of profit now that ex-slave owners
would not return to the old system if they could.

So many able writers have shown that the un-
just institutions which work so much misery and
suffering to the masses have their root in governments, and owe their whole existence to the power
derived from government, we cannot help but believe that were every law, every title deed, every
court, and every police officer or soldier abolished
tomorrow with one sweep, we would be better off
than now. The actual, material things that man
needs would still exist; his strength and skill would

remain and his instinctive social inclinations retain their force and the resources of life made free to all the people that they would need no force but that of society and the opinion of fellow beings to keep them moral and upright.

Freed from the systems that made him wretched before, he is not likely to make himself more wretched for lack of them. Much more is contained in the thought that conditions make man what he is, and not the laws and penalties made for his guidance, than is supposed by careless observation. We have laws, jails, courts, armies, guns and armories enough to make saints of us all, if they were the true preventives of crime; but we know they do not prevent crime; that wickedness and depravity exist in spite of them, nay, increase as the struggle between classes grows fiercer, wealth greater and more powerful and poverty more gaunt and desperate.

To the governing class the anarchists say: "Gentlemen, we ask no privilege, we propose no restriction; nor, on the other hand, will we permit it. We have no new shackles to propose, we seek emancipation from shackles. We ask no legislative sanction, for co-operation asks only for a free field and no favors; neither will we permit their interference.("?) It asserts that in freedom of the social unit lies the freedom of the social state. It asserts that in freedom to possess and utilize soil lie social happiness and progress and the death of rent. It asserts that order can only exist where liberty prevails, and that progress leads and never follows order. It asserts, finally, that this emancipation will inaugurate liberty, equality, fraternity. That the existing industrial system has outgrown its usefulness, if it ever had any, is, I believe, admitted by all who have given serious thought to this phase of social conditions.

The manifestations of discontent now looming upon every side show that society is conducted on wrong principles and that something has got to be done soon or the wage class will sink into a slavery worse than was the feudal serf. I say to the wage class: Think clearly and act quickly, or you are lost. Strike not for a few cents more an hour, because the price of living will be raised faster still, but strike for all you earn, be content with nothing less.

Following are definitions which will appear in all of the new standard dictionaries:

Anarchism — The philosophy of a new social order based on liberty unrestricted by man-made law, the theory that all forms of government are based on violence—hence wrong and harmful, as well as unnecessary.

Anarchy — Absence of government; disbelief in and disregard of invasion and authority

based on coercion and force; a condition of society regulated by voluntary agreement instead of
government.

Anarchist — 1. A believer in Anarchism; one
opposed to all forms of coercive government and
invasive authority. 2. One who advocates Anarchy,
or absence of government, as the ideal of political
liberty and social harmony.

2

A WORD TO TRAMPS

1884
in *The Alarm*

A word to the 30,000 now tramping the streets of this great city, with hands in pockets, gazing listlessly about you at the evidences of wealth and pleasure of which you own no part, not sufficient even to purchase yourself a bit of food with which to appease the pangs of hunger now gnawing at your vitals. It is with you and the hundreds of thousands of others similarly situated in this great land of plenty, that I wish to have a word.

Have you not worked hard all your life, since you were old enough for your labor to be of use in the production of wealth? Have you not toiled long, hard, and laboriously in producing wealth?

And in all those years of drudgery, do you not know you have produced thousand upon thousands of dollars' worth of wealth, which you did not then, do not now, and unless you act, never will, own any part in? Do you not know that when you were harnessed to a machine, and that machine harnessed to steam, and thus you toiled your ten, twelve, and sixteen hours in the twenty-four, that during this time in all these years you received only enough of your labor product to furnish yourself the bare, coarse necessaries of life, and that when you wished to purchase anything for yourself and family it always had to be of the cheapest quality? If you wanted to go anywhere you had to wait until Sunday, so little did you receive for your unremitting toil that you dare not stop for a moment, as it were? And do you not know that with all your squeezing, pinching, and economizing, you never were enabled to keep but a few days ahead of the wolves of want? And that at last when the caprice of your employer saw fit to create an artificial famine by limiting production, that the fires in the furnace were extinguished, the iron horse to which you had been harnessed was stilled, the factory door locked up, you turned upon the highway a tramp, with hunger in your stomach and rags upon your back?

Yet your employer told you that it was over-production which made him close up. Who cared for the bitter tears and heart-pangs of your loving wife and helpless children, when you bid them a loving "God bless you!" and turned upon the tramper's road to seek employment elsewhere? I say, who cared for those heartaches and pains? You were only a tramp now, to be execrated and denounced as a "worthless tramp and a vagrant" by that very class who had been engaged all those years in robbing you and yours. Then can you not see that the "good boss" or the "bad boss" cuts no figure whatever? that you are the common prey of both, and that their mission is simply robbery? Can you not see that it is the **industrial system** and not the "boss" which must be changed?

Now, when all these bright summer and autumn days are going by, and you have no employment, and consequently can save up nothing, and when the winter's blast sweeps down from the north, and all the earth is wrapped in a shroud of ice, hearken not to the voice of the hypocrite who will tell you that it was ordained of God that "the poor ye have always"; or to the arrogant robber who will say to you that you "drank up all your wages last summer when you had work, and that is the reason why you have nothing now, and the workhouse or the woodyard is too good for you; that you ought to be shot." And shoot you they will if you present your petitions in too emphatic a manner. So hearken not to them, but list! Next winter, when the cold blasts are creeping through the rents in your seedy garments; when the frost is

biting your feet through the holes in your worn-
out shoes, and when all wretchedness seems to
have centered in and upon you; when misery has
marked you for her own, and life has become a
burden and existence a mockery; when you have
walked the streets by day, and slept upon hard
boards by night, and at last determined by your
own hand to take your life—for you would rather
go out into utter nothingness than to longer en-
dure an existence which has become such a
burden—so, perchance, you determine to dash
yourself into the cold embrace of the lake rather
than longer suffer thus. But halt before you
commit this last tragic act in the drama of your
simple existence. Stop! Is there nothing you can
do to insure those whom you are about to orphan
against a like fate? The waves will only dash over
you in mockery of your rash act; but stroll you
down the avenues of the rich, and look through
the magnificent plate windows into their volup-
tuous homes, and here you will discover the *very
identical robbers* who have despoiled you and yours.
Then let your tragedy be enacted *here*! Awaken
them from their wanton sports at your expense.
Send forth your petition, and let them read it by
the red glare of destruction. Thus when you cast
"one long, lingering look behind," you can be as-
sured that you have spoken to these robbers in the
only language which they have ever been able to
understand; for they have never yet deigned to no-

tice any petition from their slaves that they were not *compelled* to read by the red glare bursting from the cannons' mouths, or that was not handed to them upon the point of the sword. You need no organization when you make up your mind to present this kind of petition. In fact, an organization would be a detriment to you; but each of you hungry tramps who read these lines avail yourselves of those little methods of warfare which Science has placed in the hands of the poor man, and you will become a power in this or any other land.

Learn the use of explosives!

Dedicated to the tramps by
Lucy E. Parsons.

3

OUR CIVILIZATION: IS IT WORTH SAVING?

August 8, 1885
in *The Alarm*

Is our civilization of today worth saving? might well be asked by the disinherited of the earth. In one respect 'tis a great civilization. History fails to record any other age like ours. When we wish to travel we fly, as it were, on the wings of space, and with a wantonness that would have sunk the wildest imagination of the gods of the ancients into insignificance. We annihilate time. We stand upon the verge of one continent, and converse with ease and composure with friends in the midst of the next. The awe-inspiring phenomena of nature concern us in this age but little. We have stolen the lightning from the gods and made it an obedient servant to the will of man; have pierced the clouds and read the starry page of time.

We build magnificent piles of architecture, whose dizzy heights dazzle us as we attempt to follow with our eye along up the towering walls of solid brick, granite and iron, where tier after tier is broken only by wondrous panes of plate glass. And as we gradually bring the eye down story after story until it reaches the ground, we discover within the very shadow of these magnificent abodes the houseless man, the homeless child, the young girl offering her virtue for a few paltry dollars to hire a little room away up in the garret of one of them. And in the dark recesses of these beautiful buildings the "tramp," demoralized by poverty and abashed by want, attempts to slink from the sight of his fellow beings.

Yet it was their labor that erected these evidences of civilization. Then why are they compelled to be barbarians? For it is labor, and labor only, which makes civilization possible. 'Tis labor that toils, and spins, and weaves, and builds, that another, not it, may enjoy. 'Tis the laborers who dive into the unknown caverns of the sea and compel her to yield up her hidden treasures, which they know not even the value thereof. 'Tis labor which goes into the trackless wilderness, and wields the magic wand which science has placed in its hand. Its hideous, hissing monsters soon succumb, and she blossoms like the rose.

Labor only can level the mountain to the plain, or raise the valley to the mountain height, and dive into the bowels of the earth and bring forth the hidden treasures there contained, which have been latent through the changing cycles of time, and with cunning hand fashion them into articles of use and luxury for the delight and benefit of mankind.

Now, why does this important factor in the arts of progress and refinement continue to hold a secondary position in all the higher and nobler walks of life? Is it not that a few idlers may riot in luxury and ease—said few having dignified themselves "upper classes"?

It is this "upper class" which determines what kind of houses (if any at all) the producing class shall live in, the quantity and quality of food they shall place upon their table, the kind of raiment they shall wear, and whether the child of the proletariat shall in tender years enter the schoolhouse or the factory.

And when the proletariat, failing to see the justice of this bourgeois economy, begins to murmur, the policeman's club is called into active service for six days in the week, while on the seventh the minister assures him that to complain of the powers that be is quite sinful, besides being a losing game, inasmuch as by this action he is lessening his chance for obtaining a very comfortable apartment in "the mansions eternal in the skies."

And the possessing class meanwhile are perfectly willing to pay the minister handsomely, and furnish the proletariat all the credit necessary for this if he will furnish them the cash for the erection of their mansions here.

Oh, working man! Oh, starved, outraged, and robbed laborer, how long will you lend attentive ear to the authors of your misery? When will you become tired of your slavery and show the same by stepping boldly into the arena with those who declare that "Not to be a slave is to dare and DO?" When will you tire of such a civilization and declare in words, the bitterness of which shall not be mistaken, "Away with a civilization that thus degrades me; it is not worth the saving?"

4

A CHRISTMAS STORY

December 26, 1885
in *The Alarm*

And here is my mail with a letter from Santa Claus who has not even forgotten me, although the halcyon days of childhood's sweet delusion have long since vanished from me. And the precious missive which the venerable old sire in his rambles through foreign lands has found and brought to me, becomes so interesting as I peruse its contents that I have determined to let the readers of *The Alarm* have the benefit of it.

The story is laid in a barbarous isle, and is the result of the very sudden advent of a shipwrecked Christian, who in return for the many kindnesses which he has received at the hands of his new neighbors, proposes to carry a few of them back with him to his own country that he may show them the benefits of a Christian civilization in order that the benighted barbarian may return to his own country and become a missionary in the cause of Christian civilization and a good government.

The little missive which Santa Claus has so kindly brought me seems to be a report of those missionaries made upon their return to their native country. The report says:

"They carried us in an easterly direction across the angry waves of the mighty ocean on the wings of a huge and beautiful sea bird (they called it a steamship) and landed us upon the verge of a great continent where nature seemed to always smile. And when we alighted from our lovely sea bird we were placed behind a horse of steel who blew and neighed and panted, impatient to start on his long journey across the wide expanding continent, and when at last he was started, he carried us with lightning speed; he whirled through valleys, across plains, and climbed the mountainside with all the ease of a giant that he was, never tiring, never flagging, but always reaching out as if in search of more land to cover; time seemed to dwindle before his onward strides, and space was annihilated."

A voice in the audience inquired: "How could he hold out?"

"Oh, he was driven by steam, a discovery which they claimed was the most wonderful ever made since their God had made the world."

The missionary continued to read the report: "On the fifth day after our starting they landed us in the heart of a magnificent city. This was about 10 o'clock a.m., and the people whom we saw moving about in such apparent ease, driving about the avenues of wealth and marts of trade in magnificent equipages, arrayed in costliest raiment, our guide informed us, were the sole owners of all those enormous structures which so amazed us; that they were in fact the sole possessors of the earth and all it contained, and lived but to enjoy. In our admiration we exclaimed, 'Mighty is the Christian Civilization! Great is their government!'" [Great sensation in the audience, and cries of 'Let's emigrate.']

"Hold on, comrades, hear us through," said the missionary, resuming: "We were shown all the wonderful sights in the arts and methods of warfare, and promised to be shown those of industry of this Christian people. We were conducted into marble halls where banquet boards were spread and lovely women came and went, fairy-like, all bespangled with precious jewels and gems of greatest worth. Their fair faces fairly beamed with contentment, ease and happiness." [Murmur in the audience: 'Mighty is the Christian Civilization!']

"As night grew on apace and sparkling wine from vine-wreathed cups was freely drunk, and toasts in quick succession were freely and hilariously offered, which ran about thus: 'Happy, contented, and prosperous are our people under the benign influence of a wisely managed and Christian Government,' and as the applause from the last toast echoed along down the granite columns of the banqueting hall which made the silken draperies quiver and fairly rent the magnificent frescoed ceiling, a strange apparition appeared and stood about midway in the hall so that none could help but see it."

"That apparition was the wretchedest of women. And from her cavernous eyes, pale flashes seemed to rise, as when the northern skies gleamed in December. And like the water's flow under December snow came a dull voice of woe from the heart's chamber:

'Ladies and gentlemen, Christian people,' said she, 'while at your banqueting board will you hear the prayer of the widow, the cry of the orphan? Without, the blinding snow falls thick and fast. Three months ago this day I, for the fifth time, became a mother, and on that very day I was made a widow and they were orphaned by my poor husband being crushed to a shapeless mass among the machinery in that man's factory (pointing to the proposer of the last toast) and I swear to you that twice these twelve hours past we have been without a morsel of food or a bit of fuel, and I am afraid to return to my wretched hovel for fear they have already perished from cold and hunger. Oh! In God's name hear their cries if not mine!'

For a moment all seemed transfixed; then a slight noise was heard, when from a recess emerged an officious person all done up in a large blue coat with brass buttons and quickly stepping up to the apparition, drew the thin, faded shawl over the pale, haggard cheeks and flashing eyes, thus stifling the cries for 'mercy.'"

Voices from the audience: "Didn't the Christians say anything?"

"Yes, they spoke for a few moments in whispers."

"What did they say?"

"Well, from the ladies side could be heard sentences like these: 'Pshaw! Such management, as to let such a creature make her way into the banqueting hall, and especially when strangers are present.'"

"Another lady of very matronly appearance spoke thus: 'Oh! Did you hear the language she used about becoming a mother? Just as though we care how many brats she had or when they were born.'"

"From the gentlemen we could hear expressions like these: 'Those fancied grievances from the improvident lower classes, in venting their supposed wrongs and annoying decent people, is becoming altogether too frequent. We must have the military well practiced in 'street riot drill,' and equipped so as to be ready to quell the first manifestation of an attempt on their part to force a recognition of the 'justness' of 'righting their alleged wrongs.'

Other gentlemen said: 'Yes, yes, you are right. We have been reading the *Tribune*'s appeal to businessmen after the Thanksgiving Day street riot drill, and I have myself been soliciting contributions from among the propertied classes, with no small success.'"

"These, and many more expressions of a like tenor could be heard from all present."

"The time having now arrived for leave-taking and a pleasant good-night, we soon left the room, and as myself and guide emerged from the magnificent building, our host seemed completely lost in praise of the 'prosperity and hospitality of a Christian people.'"

"We were about to take a cab, when my attention was attracted, and I stopped, with one foot upon the cab step, and as I did so, I discerned several of the brass-buttoned fellows before referred to forcing along as many young girls, who were weeping and declaring they would not have been 'soliciting' upon the street if they had not been driven to do so. One said her aged mother was without 'food or fuel,' and another said, 'Oh, sir, please, please let me go just this time. I swear to you I have been trying so hard to get work, but I could not, and now my landlord has served notice upon me, and myself and little children will be thrown upon the street if the rent is not paid tomorrow.'"

"On my turning to our friend, he guessed the question I was about to ask, and with an impatient wave of the hand, informed us that these persons 'were only a lot of unfortunate creatures whom we in this Christian country turn over to the authorities to be dealt with. In fact, that is mainly what we have our government for, the taking charge of the lower classes.'"

"When the Sabbath bells pealed out calling these Christians to their gorgeous temples to worship their gods, we, too, were escorted to one of them, and introduced to the minister in charge as some 'heathen who had been induced to come among us to learn the habits of a God-fearing people, that they might learn the ways of the Christian, in order that they might return to their own land and become missionaries.' The minister very sanctimoniously declared that 'we are faithful followers of the meek and lowly Jesus, who had nowhere to lay his head,' then mounted his gorgeous pulpit and took for his text words to this effect: 'That it was as difficult for a rich man to enter the kingdom of heaven as for a camel to go through the eye of a needle, unless they were very generous to the poor,' and when the contribution box was passed around it was very generously re-membered."

"One fine day, after we had been in the Christian country but a few weeks, we strolled down in the midst of the marts of trade, and as we stood and gazed in wonderment and admiration at the towering buildings, these same buildings seemed to suddenly begin to take on a different aspect, as we heard the great clock in the tower begin to strike the hour of six, and as it did so there began to stream out from all these monstrous buildings a blackening stream of people, who, as they came forth, seemed to be hurrying helter skelter in every direction, as though their very life depended upon their getting somewhere in the shortest time imaginable. These people seemed so different from those whom we had been accustomed to seeing. These last were pale-faced, care-worn and hard-worked people, who seemed to have no time nor desire to stop and enjoy the beautiful displays in the show windows as the well-dressed ones whom we had during the day seen doing so; and in this struggling mass of hurrying humanity we could see little children of tender age looking as over-worked as those more mature in years."

"While we were peering into these people's faces, trying to make out why it was they looked so different from those whom we had seen at church and at the banquet, just then our guide stepped up and told us that these people whom we now saw were 'only the working class; the lower element in our society.'"

"'Working people, did you say?' we asked. 'Then do they not build those beautiful buildings which they are coming out of?'"

"Oh, yes; we have them do the work, but we superintend it."

"Then of course they own them?"

"No. You see, it is like this: these people are the working class. It is the capitalists who own the property."

"Then, if these people are the working people as you say they are, why is it they are not owners of this property?'"

"Well, you see, it is very difficult for the heathen to understand the political economy of a Christian civilization. You see, it is like this: we employ these classes and pay them so much of their labor product, which we call wages; and of course this is a great blessing to them, for if they were not so employed by us they could not obtain the comforts of life they now enjoy."

"'But are they satisfied to simply receive wages for their work? Do they quietly submit?"

"No, not always; but we do not permit any interference on their part; we deal with them summarily." [A voice in the audience: 'What do you think of the Christian government and their boasted civilization?']

"What do we think of it? Why, from what we

could learn of their government it is simply organized fraud and oppression; because if their people are happy and contented as they claim, then what do they need to be governed for? And in their religion they are hypocrites, inasmuch as they preach one thing and practice another."

"And in their economical or industrial system they are robbers, fleecing old and young alike, and under the shadow of their altars they keep great engines of destruction that they may send their enemies to hell by the wholesale. As for my part, I move that we send missionaries among them at once, not to teach them how to die, but how to live; not to be soul-savers but body-savers. Teach them how not to make criminals of the people by overwork and poverty that their ministers may have a job praying them out of hell!"

In the midst of the great sensation and commotion which arose at this motion and the cries of "second the motion," and "send missionaries at once!"—amid all this confusion Santa Claus seems to have lost part of the manuscript of this very interesting report, and the readers of *The Alarm* will have to be content with what is here given.

5

WE ARE ALL ANARCHISTS

March 12, 1887
in *The Advance and Labor Leaf*

There is no picture so dark but has its bright side—no life so dreary but what at some time a ray of hope flits across its cheerless path. There is no movement so heinous (?) but to those engaged in it has its amusing side. But who can assume for one moment that the awful, horrible, anarchistic movement of "blood-drinking" anarchists can have any amusing side to it? How could such "fiends" ever smile? For after reading insinuations from the pulpit, assertions from the press, and "criticisms" from professional critics, to the average reader an avowed anarchistic society must be composed of beings somewhat resembling the human family, who hold orgies, which they designate as meetings; having been compelled to come in contact with the human race enough (just enough) to learn a few words of their language.

Places selected for holding said meetings (orgies) by these "anarchist fiends" are in keeping with all the rest of their diabolisms, inasmuch as they invariably select only places that are dark, dank and loathsome, where no light is ever permitted to penetrate, either of sunlight or intelligence. And at such appointed times and places these "hysterics of the labor movement" (for these "fiends" have deluded themselves into the belief that they have something in common with the labor movement) write their diabolical mandates upon grimy tables covered with bomb-slaughtered capitalists, these "fiends" having improved upon the capitalist method of starving said victims, and then taking their hides to make fine slippers for their daughters, etc.

And as these "foul conspirators" each in turn reaches a mangy hand under the table and takes therefrom a capitalistic infant's skull, each slowly raises bloodshot eyes, fills said skull with sour beer, and clinks the same with some fellow- conspirator's sour beer which is contained in the empty half of a dynamite bomb. At this signal, the whole crowd arise and straighten, as well as they can, their tatterdemalion forms, and with distended nostrils hiss from between clenched teeth, **"blood!"**

Now, I will ask the readers of The Advance and the reading public if the above picture is at all overdrawn when compared with articles from the press, both so-called religious and secular, and also of insinuations from the pulpit for the last few months, regarding that class of people designated anarchist?

The amusing part of this business to the average anarchist is just here—i.e., that we are being used just now as a kind of a bugaboo, a scarecrow to frighten the capitalists into certain concessions to their rebellious slaves, otherwise said slaves might become "anarchist fiends." And this little game is being played for all its worth by certain labor "reformers" and especially by the church. But the capitalists don't frighten a dollar's worth.

In substantiation of a thousand illustrations coming under the observation of anarchists all the time, I need here but note a few, and these from the pulpit. The Rev. Hugh O. Pentecost, of the Congregational church, Newark, N.J., in his sermon entitled the "Henry George Solution of the Labor Problem," as reported in the New York Standard, says:

If you say that Henry George is an anarchist, you will simply be exposing your own ignorance. A man who writes two or three books of a purely philosophical character is not an anarchist. A book is not an anarchist's instrument. Before you pronounce judgment on a man you want to hear what that man has to say.

Wonder if the most Rev. D.D. has ever heard of Reclus, Kropotkin, Bakunin, Proudhon, Marx, Fourier and a host of other renowned anarchists who have written books of "a purely philosophical character"? From the same sermon I take this extract:

The Roman Catholic church has made a big mistake in opposing the Knights of Labor. I have studied the Knights of Labor for several years, and I have become convinced that the organization is one of the great bulwarks that stand between society and red-handed anarchism.

Does this reverend gentleman throw this out as sop to capitalists? Yes, "bulwarks," "red-handed anarchism," etc. Well, it won't work, because the twenty-one demands of the Knights of Labor platform are an endeavor to supplant the present wage system by a system of cooperation and my dear friend, "red-handed anarchism," where and when the wage system has ended. Every attempt of labor organizations to improve the condition of the wage-worker, is—when successful—a limitation of the capitalist's power (authority) and a limitation of the severities of the wage-system.

The capitalist understands full well that his power consists solely of his privilege to dictate the terms and conditions to those who bring to him their commodity-labor-for-sale, and any organization, it matters not under what name, which attempts in any way to limit or deny this privilege, viz: the power of the possessing class over the non-possessing producing class, is met by the lockout, the blacklist, and when necessary, the policeman's club and the militiaman's bayonet. And this is all justified upon the right of the employer's "conducting his business to suit himself."

Now these are potent facts, which no one having eyes to see can deny, and to assume for one moment that capital and labor (or capitalists and laborers) have an identity of interest, is to assume that the purchaser and seller of a pair of boots have an identity of interest. The one has something to sell, the other to buy. The one's interest is to get all he can, the other's to give just as little as possible. And this commodity—labor—is controlled the same as any other article, *viz*: by the amount to be found in the market. Hence it is the capitalistic class always in all countries, who strive and manage to keep an army of laborers in compulsory idleness, to be moved around to take the place of any "kickers" in that very "bulwark" which is to stand between them and "red-handed anarchism."

Again the reverend gentleman says:

The Knights of Labor imagine that they are tyrannized over, and once in a while they will do things no one will commend them for. It is this system. A great many think the troubles arise from employers. I know some that are as good as any men who walk the face of the earth. There are some hard-hearted employers, but they are not at the bottom of the trouble. It is on account of the system.

Yes, I presume it is only imagination (?) on the part of the K. of L. that they are "tyrannized over." But it is the "system," says the reverend gentleman, which is at fault. What more has any anarchist said? Evidently, the reverend gentleman, like many others, is an anarchist and doesn't know it. But you just touch this beautiful wage system and see under what head capital will place you. And as to those "good employers," so too there were good chattel slave masters, but what did that have to do with the system of chattel slavery, except to prolong its existence by having the good slave masters held up as shining examples to prove the harmony (?) existing between master and slave, which the horrible abolitionist would sever, just as is the case today with those relations between "good" employers and the wage-slaves, which the "red-handed anarchist" is seeking to destroy. But the anarchists simply answer with the Rev. D.D., "it is the system which is at fault."

Well, if it is the system that is at the bottom of the trouble, then it certainly should follow to the average thinking person that the system must be changed. But this reverend gentleman durst not propose such a remedy to his congregation, else he might be set down as a "disturber of the peace," just as though anything in the line of justice can be brought about unless the "peace" of established injustice is disturbed!

I will state briefly for the information of those who are so busily engaged just now in declaiming against the system and declaring they are not anarchists in the same breath, that our position is about this, to-wit: The wage-system having outgrown its usefulness, inasmuch as it creates famine in the midst of abundance, and makes slaves of nine-tenths of the human family, that it (the system) must go!

And having read history I can't find any instance where the ruling classes have relinquished any "vested right" without compulsion. And knowing that private property in the means of existence is a "vested right" as much as any ever was or can be, it being upheld by the constitutions of all governments, backed by their powerful armies, we don't believe the privileged class are going peaceably to surrender these "vested rights."

6

THE FACTORY CHILD

September 10, 1905
in *The Liberator*

After reading a recent census report showing that children (white children) are toiling in the cotton factories of the South for $1.75 per week, one is constrained to inquire: Where do the burdens of capitalism press heaviest? When we see the father who has kissed his loving wife and helpless little ones an affectionate "God bless you" and turn heavily upon his heel to seek employment, he knows not where, that he may furnish them bread, he knows not how much, we are tempted to say of this man that pleasure has become to him a mockery, and misery a part of his being.

When we witness day by day the tired maiden

wearing away her young life amid the dismal din of the factory wheels, we may say, here, indeed, the system of wage-slavery must press heaviest. Yet it is not so, for the deep, dark, damnable oppressions of capitalism are felt more keenly by the young and innocent, than by the more mature in years. While some whirl through the short space which time has allotted to them here, and in one grand round of pleasure fairly dance down to their graves as it were unaware, there is a great class who cannot even say their life has been sad from the cradle to the grave, since they never experienced that luxury of childhood's innocence, a cradle; and as to a grave, why the dissecting table is quite good enough for "paupers."

When giddy laughter and wine-bibbed mirth rings out from within the soft silken-hung halls and finds its way through gilded casements and echoes along down the broad avenues of ease, it here encounters a counter echo—this last proceeding from some noisome, dark, forbidding alley where dwell the weary little toilers, where "balmy sleep" refuses to light on lids so flooded with hot, burning tears—this last echo in the wail of the factory child, whose twitching nerves, and aching limbs refuse to be calmed after the long strain of the day's drudgery. It is here, indeed, that the climax of misery and oppression has been reached.

It is the slaughtering of the innocents. It is the

coining of these little ones into precious diadems to deck "my lady's brow," that brow which was never sullied by care or want. Yet why cannot this be said of the factory child, the producer of so much wealth? O factory child, what sage has sung thy song correct? Who thy tale of misery hath half told? What tongue or pen has yet been found powerful enough to depict thy wrongs in words that could touch the callous heart, that sacrifices thy innocence to the lust of greed!

O factory child! What can be said of thee, thou wee, wan thing? 'Tis thy teardrop which flashes from the jeweled hand of the factory lord. 'Tis thy blood which colors the rubies worn in his gorgeous drawing room.

But those tears of thy young years shall not be shed in vain; thy blood will not always be crystallized on the fingers of dainty ladies. O, child of late! Have patience amid the murmurs of discontent, which will be wafted back to you on every breeze that kisses thy pale cheek in the struggle of the coming years.

Toil on, toil on, thou victim of capitalism! Some day thy tears will be dried; some day thy chest will cease to heave. For brave hearts and strong arms will annihilate the accursed system which binds you down to drudgery and death. Only then will the factory door to tender childhood be forever closed, and the schoolhouse be flung open, and all the avenues of art and

learning be opened up to children of the producing many.

Men! Producers of the world's wealth, press
on to the front! Unfurl the banner of revolution,
fling it to the breeze, and let its folds stream out to
catch the incoming breeze which whispers liberty,
fraternity, equality.

Rescue your little ones from the deep, dark,
damnable throes of capitalism. Be men! Dare
and do.

7

AMERICANS! AROUSE YOURSELVES!

September 24, 1905
in *The Liberator*

It has not been so many years ago since it was an accepted fact that this was a middle-class Republic. Hence it was immune against those upheavals that have in times past disturbed the equanimity of the "better classes" of Europe. If there are any such persons at the present time hugging these delusions we would be pleased to have them peruse the following extracts, taken from an interview with James R. Keene, of Wall Street fame. He says:

It is my firm conviction that the day is coming when the individual small merchant will cease to exist. In his place will be millions of persons working for wages and salaries whereas yesterday and today there were and are proprietors. In other words, I believe the time is coming when practically all mercantile and industrial affairs will be conducted by corporations.

Now, Americans, what are you going to do about this evil wave that is rushing in upon you and yours like an inundating flood? Are you going to stand still until it carries you off into the ocean of wage-slavery? Are there not enough there already struggling for a wretched existence?

Oh, I think I hear you say, "Why, I am going to use the ballot, the freeman's weapon, and elect good men to office, who will seize the boa constrictor-like trusts and control them. Are we not free-born American citizens?"

Oh, are you, though? Not too much assurance, please. Let us see what Alton B. Parker has to say. When asked to comment on the admission of George W. Perkins, vice-president of the New York Life Insurance Company, that Mr McCall had contributed $50,000 of the funds of the company to the Republican campaign fund last year, Mr. Parker said:

Yes, I believe I ought to say, now that there is no political excitement to distract the public attention, that the president of the New York Life was not the only such contributor. The officers of other great life insurance companies, such as the Equitable and the Mutual, also contributed from the policy-holders funds for campaign purposes last year. What has been proved in the case of the New York Life undoubtedly would be proved in the other cases. Were there an investigation of railroad, manufacturing and other corporations, it would be found that these life insurance officers were not the only corporation officers who put their hands into the treasury and took out moneys belonging to widows and orphans to help secure a partisan triumph.

That their acts were unlawful and their purposes corrupt goes without saying. Such men desire the triumph of that party which will better serve their personal financial interests and will—for contributions, past, present and future—continue to protect those interests by lenient legislation and by pretense at execution of law which shall be tenderly blind to all their offenses. That party they espouse in the boardroom, and contribute to it of the moneys they hold in trust, and, occasionally, a little of their own. . . .

The officers responsible for these raids upon the treasuries of corporations have received their reward in unfettered management of life insurance corporations; in unembarrassed raids upon the public through trusts—condemned by both common and statute law; in refusal to punish criminally the officers of railroad and other corporations violating the laws, and in statutory permission to manufacturing corporations to levy tribute on the people.

There can be no hope of checking the unlawful aggressions of officers of great corporations so long as they may thus form a quasi-partnership with the organization for the dominant political party. For, in the hour when the administration official seeks to punish the offender he is reminded by the head of the organization of the magnitude of the contributions of the corporation.

There is, however, something worse, if possible, than the escape of such offenders from justice. It is the gradual demoralization of voters and the dulling of the public conscience caused by the efforts to make these vast sums of money procure the ballots they were intended to procure, corruptly and otherwise.

Reader, have you read the above carefully? Yes? Then we ask you again: What are you going to do about it? Forty years ago a wail came up from the Sunny South that 4,000,000 black slaves were held in bondage. The eloquent Wendell Phillips, William Lloyd Garrison and many others depicted the auction block, the wail of innocent childhood, the anguish of womanhood who were compelled to do their master's bidding. It is not quite so bad in the North today, it is true, but how many of the wage class, as a class, are there who can avoid obeying the commands of the master (employing) class, as a class? Not many, are there?

Then are you not slaves to the money power as much as were the black slaves to the Southern slaveholders? Then we ask you again: What are you going to do about it? You had the ballot then. Could you have voted away black slavery? You know you could not because the slaveholders would not hear of such a thing for the same reason you can't vote yourselves out of wage-slavery.

The trusts will not allow you to vote them out of power because they are the power, as is shown by the interview given above.

All that the master class care for is to rush their "hands" through the factory grist, get all there is of strength and vitality out of them to pay interest on their watered stock, and when they are practically exhausted, then turn them over to the tender mercies of their police, to be "run in" as vagrants.

This is the fate which awaits many of the middle class and the wage-class. What are you going to do about it? Are you going to serve notice on these thieves, and highway robbers, sitting in high places of "honor" and "trust," that by the eternal god of justice, and by the manhood in you, that you will not, in this land of plenty, allow your children to become the mere hirelings and dependents upon the sweet will of their children?

Remind them that the sword still hangs upon the wall and the heart still beats within the man, and that that sword will be unsheathed again, if necessary, in defense of your rights. Give them to understand that you will not stand patiently by and see your hard earnings squandered by a luxuriating class of idlers. If the American manhood will arouse itself and speak to those fellows in plain language, not to be misunderstood, they can save themselves, their country and their children, from the fate of poverty which awaits them.

Will you do it?

8

WHAT FREEDOM MEANS

October 8, 1905
in *The Liberator*

The change from the present method of obtaining one's living is inevitable, because it has become a necessity. We now live under the pay system, in which if you can't pay you can't have. Everything has a price set upon it; earth, air, light and water, all have their price. And he who hasn't worked, let him starve. Love, honor, fame, ambition, all the noblest and holiest aspirations and sentiments of humanity are bought and sold. Everything is upon the market for sale; all is merchandise and commerce. Land, the prime necessity of existence, is held for a price, and the homeless millions perish because they cannot pay for it. Food, raiment and shelter exist in super-abundance, but are withheld for the price.

The productive and distributive forces of nature, united with the power and ingenuity of man are reserved for a price. And humanity perishes from disease, crime and ignorance because of its enforced, artificial poverty. The mental, moral, intellectual and physical qualities are dwarfed, stunted and crushed to maintain the price. This is slavery, the enslavement of man to his own powers: Can it continue? The change is inevitable because necessary. Free access to all the productive and distributive forces will alone free the minds and bodies of men. There are certain things that are priceless. Among these are life, liberty and happiness, and these are the things which the society of the future, the free society, will guarantee to all for the return of a few hours labor per day.

When labor is no longer for sale, society will produce free men and women, who will think free, act free, and be free. Crime and criminals will flee from such a society, because the incentive for crime will be gone.

9
ANARCHISM

February 3, 1906
in *The Liberator*

We are told that the word Anarchy needs constant explanation; that whenever used in its literal sense it must be defined. Is there any other word of which this is not true? The introduction of new ideas into a man's mind is not accompanied by the use of a specially coined word, but by the adaptation of old words to broader uses. Even the word self-government would not convey our meaning in its broadest generalization. This word has been understood since its introduction into general use to mean a system of representative government—the delegation of personal rights to be represented by another person deemed to be the highest approach of liberty possible in a state.

In seeking the establishment, not of a system of government, but of the greater extension of liberty, the use of this word would be far more objectionable than the word Anarchy, and this because it carries with it a recognition of government and the necessity of political action; Earl Derby boasted when Premier in the House of Lords of England's "principles of popular government."

In every instance in which Americans use the word "self-government" it carries with it the idea of representation as well as administration. States in the Union by their "residuary rights" possess self-government, and individuals enjoy the fullest self-government; the trouble is, liberty has not yet acquired a substantive tutelage of past ages, has not been outgrown so largely, but that the halo of authority still lingers around all our words.

Nevertheless, humanity tends always more and more toward individualism, that is toward real self-government, which is the only true, just and sane government. Today we are passing out of political into economic problems, over which the state has no influence, being the creature of existing economic conditions; hence, a word is needed which, while not condemning administration, will unequivocally express opposition to political government. The old bottles answered to hold the old wine of politics. Economic questions, not being solvable by political methods, demand new bottles for the new ideas time evolves.

Government is stationary, social growth is progressive; consequently we find ourselves arrived at a point where governments become a barrier to economic progress. True, this position is a reversal of the common accepted belief, which is that government is a help to progress. But a close study of the origin, tendency and operations of all governments will show that they never lead to progress.

Governments always stand for the "established order of things." Hence, we use the word anarchy, the negative of government, and will retain it when the political state has merged into the social commonwealth.

THE EIGHT HOUR STRIKE
OF 1886

May 1, 1912
in *Industrial Worker*

The Industrial Workers of the World is the last child born of the great surging struggle in the world's arena between labor and capital. It is a child vigorous and aggressive, gaining in strength, expanding in power, and commanding attention and respect. This young child is the progeny of a long line of the Earth's stalwarts who have engaged in the onward march towards a better world.

The IWW is urging the workers to set aside the first of May, 1912 to demand of the master class an eight—hour working day. Of course if the working class are not sufficiently awake to their own interests to come out and stand like men for this very just and modest demand, the IWW will not abandon the agitation; on the contrary, it may agitate for a still shorter work day, so as to keep pace, to some extent at least, with the advance in labor—saving (labor—destroying) machinery. A reduction of the working time is the most just and practical palliative that can be injected into the issue between labor and capital. In fact, while it seems to be a palliative on the face of it, it is in reality not a palliative at all, but a revolutionary measure, because time is the greatest factor in our existence.

It has taken eons of time to develop every particle of matter in the universe, man included, yet time to man is so short and precious. There is so little that he can accomplish between the time that his mother implants her first mother—love kiss upon his newborn cheek to when death has clasped him in its cold embrace. If he has run his two— or three—score years between the cradle and the grave, and has occupied every moment of that time to the very best advantage possible, he has accomplished very little indeed.

It would be well if the working class would heed the call of the IWW and cease to labor on the first day of May and take stock of themselves and try to realize what space of time elapses from the time they offer their labor to the boss, at about fifteen yearsâ€"in other words, when they place their capital on the market, "capital" which consists of stored—up power in their muscles and brainsâ€"to their forty—fifth or fiftieth year, when the best there was in them has been used up by the boss and they are flung out upon the human scrap—heap as useless material, with nothing more to be ground out of them for the benefit of the boss.

I say it will be well for them to stop for one day at least, and take stock of their stockâ€"that is of themselves, and see if it is worth while for them to spend three—fourths of their time toiling for a bare existence: not for a living, for the vast majority of them do not live, they barely exist. If they should stop to think they would soon better their condition.

The first great strike of America for a reduction of hours of labor to eight per day occurred on May First, 1886. In October 1885, a convention of labor organizations was held in Chicago; at said convention a resolution was passed, requesting the working class to set aside the First of May, 1886, to demand a reduction of the hours of the workers to eight. The Knights of Labor was not represented at the above mentioned convention and did not participate in the strike as a national organization, but many of the [Knights'] "Assemblies" did so. The radical element in Chicago were divided as to what position they should take regarding the proposed strike, some taking the position that it was only a palliative at best, that it was not worth such a gigantic struggle as must be engaged in, if it was to succeed.

Following is part of an interview by Albert R. Parsons printed in the Chicago Daily News, March 13, 1886:

The movement to reduce the work—hours is intended by its projectors to give a peaceful solution to the difficulties between the capitalists and laborers. I have always held that there were two ways to settle this trouble, either by peaceable means or violent methods. Reduced hours, or eight—hours, is the peace—offering. Fewer hours mean more pay. Reduced hours is the only measure of economic reform which consults the interests of the laborers as consumers. Now, this means a higher standard of living for the producers, which can only be acquired by possessing and consuming a larger share of their own product. This would diminish the profits of the labor exploiters.

The Central Labor Union of Chicago, consisting of 25,000 German trades unionists, passed a resolution, requesting August Spies, editor of the Arbeiter—Zeitung (German daily), and Albert R. Parsons, editor of The Alarm (English weekly), to advocate in their paper and speeches, the eight—hour day. This settled the controversy: Parsons, Spies and all the active revolutionary spirits in Chicago went to work in earnest. The result of their activities was made manifest, for when the first of May, 1886 arrived, it found Chicago the best organized city in America. In this city the working class struck between 50,000 and 60,000 strong and tied up the city more completely than I have ever seen it tied up during the thirty years that I have been a resident here.

On the afternoon of May 3rd, there were large numbers of strikers in the Southwestern portion of Chicago, among them the McCormick Reaper Works' employees. According to the capitalist papers there was rioting among them. The police were called out to quell the riots. As is usually the case, when the police were called out, the working people were sticking together in large numbers; [though the police] did manage to quell some of them. On this occasion, they shot seven working men and clubbed many hundreds unmercifully.

The next evening the Haymarket meeting was called. The Haymarket meeting is referred to historically as the "The Haymarket Anarchists' Riot." There was no riot at Haymarket except a police riot.

Mayor Carter Harrison attended the Haymarket meeting, and took the stand at the Anarchist trial for the defense, not for the state. The Mayor testified that he attended the Haymarket meeting as the highest peace official in Chicago for the purpose of dispersing it, should it require his attentions as such. The Mayor further testified that when the meeting was about to be adjourned, he went to the Desplaines Street police station, and ordered the inspector to send his reserves to their several beats as the meeting was adjourning, was peaceable, and that he the Mayor was on his way home. No sooner was the Mayor out of sight, than the inspector, who wished to do something officious at the time of the great strike, rushed a company of police upon the meeting that had practically adjourned. At the onrush of the police, someone threw a bomb. Who threw that bomb, no one to this day knows, save he who threw it. He has never been found.

But the capitalist class didn't care whether they found the bomb thrower or not; what they wanted was the leaders of the great strike, to get them out of the way and to frighten the slaves back to work. And the scheme worked magnificently, for after the bomb was thrown, the slaves for the most part forgot they had a grievance. Of course, to give the barest outline of the trial and death of my husband and comrades, would make this letter entirely too long. But the key to why their lives were sacrificed is found in the following excerpts from State's Attorney Grinnell's address to the jury. He said:

Gentlemen of the jury, these defendants at the bar are not more guilty than the thousands who follow them. They have been selected and indicted by the grand jury because they are leaders, convict them and save our society.

The great strike of May 1886, was an historic event of great importance, inasmuch as it was, in the first place, the first time that workers themselves had attempted to get a shorter work day by united, simultaneous action. To be sure there had been some earlier agitation, but always among the politicians in legislative halls and in congress. Needless to say such agitation was of no avail. But this strike was the first in the nature of Direct Action on a large scale, the first in America. It had its lasting effects, because it broke through the stone wall of the long—hour custom. What was gained by the workers was never wholly lost. The hours of labor have never been as long, as a whole, since 1886, as they were before that time.

Of course the eight—hour day is as antiquated as the craft unions themselves. Today, we should be agitating for a five—hour work day, or six at the most, but the IWW, I presume, has taken up the eight—hour cause on the principle that we must not get too far away from those we wish to influence or our labors are wasted.

The worldwide unrest among the wage class is the most hopeful sign of the times. Labor is learning that its most powerful and effective weapon is in its muscles and its brains. Let it withdraw these and the capitalist system is paralyzed. What labor wants is land for the landless, produce

to the producer, tools to the toiler and death to
wage—slavery.

    Thine oppressor's hand recoils,
    When thou. weary of thy toil,
    Shun'st thy plough, thy task begun.
    When thou speak'st: Enough is done.

Copyright © 2024 by FV Editions
Cover design and layout : FVE

Picture : Portrait of Lucy Parsons, taken at the second annual
convention of the International Labor Defense convention,
where she was the guest of honor, 1927, Labadie Photograph
Collection, University of Michigan. LPF.0864, http :
https://commons.wikimedia.org/wiki/File:Lucy_-
Parsons.1920.jpg

Ebook ISBN 979-10-299-1732-5
Paperback ISBN 979-10-299-1733-2
All rights reserved.

www.ingramcontent.com/pod-product-compliance
Lightning Source LLC
Chambersburg PA
CBHW051303160726
47994CB00003B/1290